# *Mom*

## TRENT WESTEN

PAGE PUBLISHING
Conneaut Lake, PA

First originally published by Page Publishing 2023

ISBN 979-8-88793-703-8 (pbk)
ISBN 979-8-88793-741-0 (digital)

Printed in the United States of America

# *Introduction*

I want to do more than write dull pages of black and white. Give me words that come out of the blue, colorful words to extol my mother's virtue. Let them be like the stars that come out at twilight to glorify the night.

My mother had more influence on me and bestowed more blessings upon me than any other person in the world. She was my gravitational field and my aurora borealis. Without her, I would have been like the planet without a star, dark and cold and spinning out of control. Were I the moon, then she was the earth. Were I the earth, then she was the sun. Were I the sun, then she was the Milky Way. No one else came close—not as close as a comet—to showering me with such love.

Her story begins as she swings me aboard the school bus and ends as I scatter her ashes across the desert floor. It is the story of a woman who does unto others as she would have others do unto her, but doesn't count on it. She does what she does from the goodness of her heart and expects nothing in return. She jokes that she is the maid, the butler, and the chauffeur, but that is no joke and has the elbow grease to prove it.

If a yardstick could measure love, then it would show that she got the short end of the stick. She loved me more than she loved herself and did more for me than she did for herself. She gave me too much and let me get away with too much. Her love was as boundless and as bewildering as the universe.

# Upsy-Daisy

With one big "upsy-daisy," Mom swung me aboard the school bus. My sister had already climbed up on her own. As the bus left, Mom hopped into the car and followed us—stop by stop—all the way to school. After K ran off to class, Mom drove me back home. I was too young for school, but old enough to want to ride the bus.

A decade later, I entered prep school. We lived fifteen miles from the academy—too far for the bus. Mom dropped me off in the morning and picked me up in the afternoon. She did that five days a week—three hundred miles a week—all to further my education.

Although she furthered my education without hesitation, I had little yearning for all the learning. I put my ZZZs before my ABCs and earned more Cs than As and Bs. Even the three Rs did not spark, kindle, or ignite that flame, that fire, that burning desire.

Had I dropped out of school and landed in jail, my mother would have posted bail only to hold me and never let me go.

# Stevedore

Neptune brought the sound and the silence, the calm and the violence. He brought the breaking wave, the crash, the roar, the seething surf speeding to shore. He brought the to-and-fro of the seaweed below, like the seven seas that ebb and flow.

When I was three or four, we had a boat, a dock, and a jet-black Labrador. Every day, the sea brought good tidings. Every day brought music to our door. As Jetsy lapped up water from his bowl, our boat pitched in with all its rock and roll. Even the dock knew the score, creaking like a seasaw.

Neptune lured me with legend and lore, with mermaids and Sirens and pirates galore. I heard tales from the high seas to the sea floor, but from Davy Jones's locker I heard no more.

Bait and tackle had plenty of play as we pulled bluefish from their schools, chowder clams from their beds, and blue-claw crabs from flats of mud and clay. We also caught fluke and flounder, bottom fish flatter than rounder. One day, Dad landed a fifteen-pounder. That was large for a fluke and even larger for a flounder, but not as large as the one that got away in a tug-of-war on the Great South Bay.

Our food came from coast to coast and from shore to shore, more by teamster than by stevedore. On track and on time, it came by freight train and by airline. Fresh, frozen, or canned, it came by air, sea, and land. From the city or from the sticks—like Mom's cakes—it was a mix.

We had plenty of thick cuts and plenty of thin slices, plenty of French pastries, and plenty of Italian ices. Chinese or south of the border, it was ours to order. From the corner market to the salty seas, we had plenty of good and plenty of goodies. We also had seeds to sow and a garden to grow, crows to scare, and tomatoes to share.

# The Apple of My Pie

The kitchen was our Grand Central Station. We tracked through all day long. It was also Mom's station, her shop, her stage, her show. She could pull a roast out of the oven or a rabbit out of the hat and do it right on schedule, like the trains that pulled out of Grand Central Station.

In the sixties, we didn't know which side our bread was buttered on. We traded butter for margarine only to learn that the trans fat was a transgression. Our white bread—the white wonder—turned out to be a whitewash. Even the salt of the earth turned deadly.

We saved grace for special occasions, not for daily bread. It didn't take long, and it didn't take long to fall from grace. I ate what I wanted and as much as I wanted and never had a second thought after a second serving. Seconds, of course, were a matter of course and had at every course. I thought no more about counting calories than about counting my blessings, no more about hunger than about the hungry.

Hunger never hung over me like a dark cloud. It never wore on me like the rain or waged war like a hurricane. Unlike the heat and the humidity, it didn't stick with me. Even hunger's headwinds stayed away. Plenty of home sweet home cooking held desire's storm at bay.

Along with three squares a day, Mom provided a well-rounded selection of cookies, cakes, and pies. Her cakes were heavenly, and her pies were divine. Even her cookies were out of this world. They had me as full as the full moon. Unlike the moon, I waned much slower than I waxed.

Around food I was all ears. While clanging pots and pans brought music to my ears, the laughter of children and the song of birds fell on deaf ears. The dinner bell called me to the table, and the horn of plenty was my Gabriel. Like a wooden spoon and a mixing bowl, they stirred my soul.

Every winter, I fell head over heels for pineapple upside-down cake. Come spring, my fancy turned to strawberry shortcake made with fresh berries and real whipped cream. In the summer, peach cobbler called my name. With fall, the fruit of our apple tree became the apple of my eye and the apple of my pie.

Battered by cake? Crumbling for crumb cake? Long for shortcake? Coffeecake keeping you awake dreaming of layer after layer of layer cake? Had enough, but wanted more? Wanted more than just another petit four? Cake was all that and so much more. More than cookies and more than pies, cake took the cake. Cake won the prize.

In the field of nutrition, the fruits and the vegetables remained the undisputed champions. They saw me through thick and thin, were my heroes and my heroines. They were not, however, exactly kissing cousins. According to the buzz coming from the garden, they really got under one another's skin.

The fruits were in a jam and the vegetables in a stew. The vegetables claimed that the fruits had descended from the forbidden fruit, that man was still fallen and the fruits were still falling—on the vegetables—and that was the pits. It was high time for the fruits to stop hanging around. The time was ripe for them to turn over a new leaf—a fig leaf.

The fruits took the vegetables with a grain of salt. The potatoes had eyes but could not see, and the corn had ears but could not hear. On the contrary, the fruits had the dirt on the vegetables. From their bird's-eye view, they could tell that the lettuces had been sleeping around—sharing the same bed—and that was just the tip of the iceberg.

# Triumph

Lou Levey put bread on the table, and his daughter put peanut butter on the bread. It was her meat. She was not vegetarian by choice, but by default. Meat was an extravagance at the Levey household, and she had little choice. She had little choice and little prime, little select, and little to select.

Growing up a Levey, my mother had few longings and few belongings. She was proud of what she wore and proud of what she wore out, proud of the company that she kept and too proud to let herself go. Her hourglass physique stood the test of time and lasted a lifetime.

As the daughter of a factory worker and a child of the Great Depression, she learned early on that money made the world go round, and sometimes the wheels came off. The stock market crash of 1929 wrecked the economy. Main Street hit the skids, and

Wall Street hit a brick wall. Down and out and on the street, Wall Street was up against the wall.

My mother grew up watching the silver screen only to watch her dreams of Tinseltown fold like a silver certificate. Although she never became a star, she would be the sun and the moon to me, and I meant the world to her.

As the country turned from the Great Depression to World War II—turned from a sea of red ink to a sea of blood—millions turned from the bread line to the front line. Millions more turned to the assembly line. America's military might erupted like a volcano. Planes filled the sky. Bombs shook the earth. Tanks flowed like lava.

The Cold War followed the hot war like a chill that followed a fever. Cold-blooded generals with bone-chilling weapons brought the world to a new low. They sent shivers around the world. Like a pandemic, the whole world went from hot to cold.

High blood pressure kept my father out of the service but not out of the office. As the US and the USSR engaged in the arms race, Dad engaged in the rat race. He fixed teeth as the superpowers armed to the teeth. As the adversaries practiced death and destruction, Dad built his practice. He installed bridges as the combatants burned their bridges behind them.

To dive into a drop of water or drink in a sea of stars, I had a microscope and a telescope. My sister had more changes than a kaleidoscope. We lived in a split-level house with a pool in the back and a TV in almost every room. The only thing missing, according to Mom, was a phone in the bathroom.

Love was also missing, but love came and went, a castaway in life's day-to-day. The friendship, the companionship, the partnership were all lost—overboard like flotsam and jetsam from a sinking ship. After fifteen years, my parents were breaking up. Their marriage was on the rocks.

After the Cadillac left—after Mom, K, and I were on our own—we went from a Ford Fairlane to a Thunderbird to a Triumph, which was a failure. The British sports car was trouble from the start—when it did start.

I rushed home after school and waited on the front lawn the day that Mom picked up our new car from the dealer. As she approached, I noticed that she had difficulty shifting gears—in more ways than one. As she drove up, I watched her dab away the tears.

The Triumph was my idea. Mom sacrificed the bird for me. She gave up a big V-8 for a puny four, something that just didn't add up, even with four-on-the-floor. She turned in power steering for manual—another wrong turn. The convertible top turned out to be manual as well, a tentlike affair with more folds than a road map and better left up.

Mom traded down, not up. She traded power and prestige for a buggy ride that sandwiched her in like a grilled cheese. It took some getting used to, like an English accent, but before long Mom triumphed over the Triumph. In the end, she drove it like a pro. Even her shifts were second nature—automatic.

Mom was such a good sport. If she ever regretted exchanging her comfort for a suspension that felt like a buckboard on a washboard, regretted bucket seats that had her ready to bail, regretted a jump seat that brought passengers to their knees, she never said a word—only her next car was a Ford.

# Street Smarts

Mom had no BA, no MA, and no PhD, not from UCLA or NYU or XYZ. Her education came in degrees, not in a degree. It came in ones and twos, but not one-two-three. Mom watched her p's and q's and paid her IOUs. She dotted her i's and crossed her t's, learned her ABC's and avoided SOBs.

Mom never went to college, but had plenty of class. Children surrounded her. Strangers smiled at her. Young men fell for her. When she walked into a room, she brought a breath of fresh air. When she left, she left a vacuum. Call her a course in chemistry and a lesson in physics. Call her a class act.

Although no scholar, Mom had her share of street smarts. The school of hard knocks gave her a crash course—an accelerated program—in the ways of the world. Her only tuition was intuition, and she quickly learned to read between the lines. Once around the block, she knew where & where not to cut corners. She also knew that every time she cut a corner, she made two more.

Mom did more than drive defensively, more than glance at the rear and side view mirrors, more than watch the car in front of the car in front of her. Fast lane or Main Street, Mom steered clear of trouble. She knew that the police came after the fact and the lawyers came after the money.

# The Shadow of Gaudí

The food court at the Boulevard Mall served up a slice of life as well as a slice of pizza. It dished out a local side of Vegas along with a side of fries. Although the fast-food outlet did not have much glitter or glamour or glitz, it did have plenty of glaze.

Mom often had a side of white rice, and I had black beans. They were satisfying and delicious, and I finished the short order in short order. I never spilled the beans, but it didn't take long for the musical fruit to sing.

As vegetarians, we were not very strict. Mom ate some fish, had turkey at Thanksgiving, and, as a guest, did not pick and choose. Mom was a Vegan, not a vegan.

Mom gave up coffee years ago, after drinking it for years. She gave up coffee but not the cafe, not the croissant, and not the conversation. They provided some consolation. She missed the bean and the caffeine, the sugar and cream. She missed the stimulation. She tried decaf and diet soda, but they were not her cup of tea. Even that she left half empty. She resorted to bottled water, but it didn't do anything for her.

Way back when Mom worked private duty at Cook County General, coffee and cigarettes mingled as freely as doctors and nurses. Shoulder to shoulder at the local lunch counter, strangers sat sipping coffee and sucking smoke. Smoke crossed their food and their faces, seasoned their food and their faces. It curled about their lips, their nostrils, their eyes. Smoke entered their fiber as well as their fibers. It didn't quit.

Although Mom didn't smoke, she put up with it. One day, however, she spoke up. The gentleman seated beside her held his cigarette so close to her that she could neither breathe nor eat.

She did not ask him to put it out, of course, but did request that he move it away from her. Well, he slowly turned and replied that he would gladly switch hands…if he could. Mom looked over, mortified. He only had one hand.

Mom blinked once, and a dozen years went by. She blinked again, and a dozen more were gone.

After the divorce, after the nest emptied, after the house sold—after the centrifugal years dispersed what the centripetal years had gathered—freedom loomed as large as the horizon, and responsibility fit into a suitcase. Mom packed her bags and followed her heart to live abroad and learn a second language.

Mom traveled Europe before settling in Barcelona. To help make ends meet, she landed a position as an instructor at a language institute. Ironically, she spent more time teaching English than learning Spanish. In the end, she could still roll her eyes better than her r's.

During my short stay in the seaport city, we had tapas at five and paella at ten. In the morning, Mom would scrub a ripe tomato across one or two warm corn tortillas before burying them under an avocado avolanche. Now she was talking.

At the old market along Las Ramblas, lamb hung like coats—sans coats. In the shade of the jacaranda and the shadow of Gaudí, we fell for flan. On the waterfront, the visiting Soviet navy dined on borscht as we lunched on gazpacho—a kinder, gentler cold war.

# What?

In a world of appearances, Mom knew a poor man who concealed his poverty and a rich man who concealed his wealth. She knew another man who fit into his surroundings and stood out from them. She also knew that clothes made the man, and women made the clothes. She knew that the bigger the front, the bigger the back.

Although seeing was believing, Mom knew that yes-men were no men. They could be counted but not counted on. She knew that the man with the X-ray vision got more than he had counted on. He won the prize but lost his eyes. Life didn't always measure up. Sometimes it fell short, and sometimes it was just too much.

## MOM

In all the back-and-forth, Mom took two steps forward and one step back. She put her best foot forward and watched her step. But Mom took life's ups and downs in stride. She knew that even day broke and night fell.

# Ours

As a young street vendor, I cared little for the legal tender. I yearned for someone to have and to hold. I yearned for a rainbow, not a pot of gold. Had I the sun and the moon and the stars, I'd have had nothing 'til they were ours.

Radio in the sand, music in the air, lovers hand in hand, romance was everywhere. Even the fog that turned my navy-blue town battleship gray, covered the land like lingerie.

While one woman had my ear, another woman caught my eye only to have another turn my head until another took my breath away. Oh! How I was taken by those knock-kneed beauties. Love really had a hold on me, really had me in the palm of her hand. There was a magic to love that not even science could explain. Ironically, we called it chemistry.

## Alarm

When the moon was made of green cheese and I was made of snips and snails and puppy-dog tails, Mom made like the Big Bad Wolf and made me laugh.

With arms akimbo, she huffed and puffed and pretended to blow down our house. Back then, her exhalations filled me with delight. Now, her exhalations filled me with alarm.

If Mom had been at rest when I called, if she had been watching TV or reading, her breathing remained silent; but if she had been active, if she had just climbed the flight of stairs to her apartment or had been cleaning house, she sounded winded—too winded.

I heard no labored breathing while in her presence, only over the phone. The phone picked up her breath as well as her words. Over time, I focused more on her breath than on her words. Her breath imparted more than her words, in volumes without a word. Next to that ill wind, her words were mere leaves in the wind.

The change in her health dawned slowly and dawned on her slowly. As subtle as the dawn, it tiptoed in like the dawn. Little by little, though, her illness replaced her health until—at the end of the day—her health had tiptoed away.

# The New Ritz of Glitz

Vegas grew fast, boomtown fast. It was America's fastest-growing city, busy turning vacant land into vacancies. Along Las Vegas Boulevard, hotels lined up like a chorus line—with more about to kick in. Rome wasn't built in a day, but Paris, Monte Carlo, New York-New York all sprang up overnight.

Like the Nevada Test Site to the north, Vegas had reached critical mass. The population was exploding, construction booming, tourism soaring. At night, Vegas glowed for miles around.

After the sun went down and the desert cooled down, Vegas heated up. As hot as Vegas was during the day, at night Vegas was hotter than hot. Vegas was on fire. Fortunes made over a lifetime elsewhere were made overnight in Vegas. At night, those denizens of the dark—gamblers—came out like stars in the desert sky. The moon shined and the stars sparkled, but Vegas electrified.

Mom lived in Vegas for twenty years and had seen casinos come and go like Lady Luck, but the arrival of the Bellagio was a defining moment in a city that lived for the moment.

Shortly before the grand opening, we drove by for a gander. We parked up ahead at New York-New York and walked back toward Bellagio under blue skies, white clouds, and a red-hot sun. We walked back under the red, white, and blue. Soon Mom was flagging.

Mom did well in the cactus clime as she swung from solstice to solstice. She did well in winter's low and well in summer's high—until lately. Now as the sun beat down on her happy trails, it beat up on her.

We hadn't gotten very far before Mom suddenly fell silent. She stood breathless. Would that the Bellagio had taken her breath away, but she stood gasping for air. She stood with one hand drawn across her breast and shock scrawled across her face, but stood her ground.

Mom suffered a seizure that morning, one far more insidious than the petty theft common along the Strip. Unlike a purse snatched or a wallet lifted, hers was an inside job. Hike and heat and heart all had a hand in her heist.

Although her breath returned in moments, there was no turning back. The die had been cast. Death had come a knocking. He did not enter, but he did post notice.

# Bellagio

The Bellagio Hotel and Casino opened on October 15, 1998. Wild deuces couldn't keep Mom away. Located in the heart of the Strip, Bellagio quickly became the heart of the Strip. From smart shops and class acts to fine dining and fine art finer than fine gold, Bellagio didn't miss a beat.

As the shining star in a cluster of stellar properties, the five-star resort had Mom starstruck. A Steve Wynn production, Bellagio promised masterpiece after masterpiece—including Monet and Matisse and Megabucks. By any measure, Bellagio promised to be a Wynner.

Bellagio opened like a flower. High roller and hoi polloi swirled about from stem to stamen. Oohs and aahs fell like petals. In the main lobby, a garden of glass flowers rose to the occasion. The giant blooms hung from the ceiling of the Italian-inspired hotel. Handcrafted in Italy, they also remained true to their roots.

A beeline away, the glass-domed conservatory had row after row of chrysanthemum. It had a ton of them. The mum multitudes were gathered before a horn of plenty as tall as a cornfield, a cornucopia of enormous yield. The conical receptacle provided quite the spectacle as it showed off nature's bounty even in Clark County, showed off what the earth had given and man had gotten without box or carton.

The cucurbits or gourd family came out in force, having poured from the massive horn like soldiers from a Trojan horse. There were cucumbers and melons and squashes and gourds from short to tall—warts and all. The harvest landslide tumbled far and wide. Pumpkins broader than a man's shoulders were strewn about like boulders.

A bumblebee flight away, the casino was as busy as a beehive. The tables were humming, the players all abuzz. Instead of flowerpots, there were jackpots. Instead of honeybees, there were wannabees. With any luck, like bees laden with pollen, a little gold dust would rub off on them too.

The lions were proud at the MGM Grand, and trapeze artists wowed the crowd at Circus Circus, but nothing stole the show like the dancing fountains at Bellagio.

In a region as dry as gin, they were more than a tonic. They were the toast of the town, and thousands came to drink them in. They came to give a listen and take a look, to belly up to the sparkling chapter of the thirty-six-story storybook.

Some rode the elevator down. Others drove from miles around. But whether they came in heels or on wheels, they came night and day to watch Bellagio's twelve-acre lake erupt into a water ballet.

Cars stopped and jaws dropped along the Strip as jets of water let it rip. In the blink of an eye, they rocketed a dozen stories high. Like a bird on the wing or a kite on a string, they could swivel and sway any which way in a dazzling display of splendor and spray.

# Leaving San Diego

San Diego to Las Vegas was not much more than two mountain passes and the desert between, not much more than a hop, skip and a jump. Although the drive from the Golden State to the Silver State amounted to spare change for most cars, mine gave it all it had. I climbed the passes and crossed the desert in an old jalopy and crossed myself as well.

Leaving San Diego was an uphill battle, one hill at a time. I-15 went up and down like a yo-yo diet of weight lost and found, but the real fight was the traffic. It got heavier by the day.

The interstate was the new Wild West—north, south, east, and west. Like gunslingers of the Old West, too many drivers took too many chances one too many times. Speeders threw caution to the wind—like litter. On the way to Vegas, they took drinks in hand—along with their lives—and lost everything before playing their first hand.

The freeway was not free. It took a terrible toll. Accidents came a mile a minute, at breakneck speed. Road kill was an unspoken tragedy. Flora, of course, got the brush. Even the land received the cold shoulder—both of them.

Man made the road and the rules of the road, but Mother Earth set the ground rules. She laid down the law of the land. Her earthquakes were part of the land and parted the land long before man paved over the land. The movers and shakers were as old as the hills—the rolling hills.

Long before the city and long before the state and long before the interstate that linked city and state, the San Andreas Fault made the impassable passable. It moved mountains and made the Cajon Pass. The pass broke the age-old impasse separating the coastal region from the high desert, but more ages would pass before I-15 piggybacked on the pass to link the City of Angels and Sin City via mountains that linked heaven and earth.

Up, down, right, left, I-15 rode the ancient cleft. From the base, it climbed like an eagle. From the summit, it dropped like a hawk. Cars and trucks had a magic carpet ride. Crossing wildlife committed suicide.

Santa Ana winds blew through Cajon Pass and blew hard. They could deck a big rig with just one blow or turn the native chaparral into a smoldering inferno. Following hot on the heels of the hot and dry summers, hot and dry Santa Anas could shake an RV like a baby rattle or drive a wildfire like a stampede of cattle.

The seasonal winds cut through Cajon Pass, but McDonald's had it all sewn up. The fast-food giant had the only eatery in sight. There wasn't a pancake house or taco shop as far as the eye could see—not a billboard. Any way you sliced it, Mickey D's made the grade.

Two hundred miles of desert separated Cajon Pass from Mountain Pass. I crossed the sea of sand in an old boat, a washed-up Chrysler that ran like a boat. On the highway, she floated like a boat. On surface streets, she hit bottom like a boat. The eighteen-footer had the turning radius of a boat and a big V-8 that guzzled gas like a boat. In a downpour, she took on water like a boat. No doubt about it, Detroit built one hulluva boat.

My first drive to Vegas was in the driving rain. Had I known better, I'd have taken a plane—better to fly over the Great Basin than circle the drain. It rained so hard that Christmas Eve, it was hard to believe. I never did see Santa's sleigh, though I spotted Noah's ark along the way—through a periscope, I dare say.

# Fremont Street

Back in the day, Vegas turned a blind eye to organized crime, and Vegas paid the price. It spent the day with one eye shut and slept with one eye open. The long arm of the law was in bed with the strong arm of the outlaw and the greased hand in the pocket of the heavy hand. First they lined their pockets, then they stuffed them.

Mob rule came and went, but the wink and the nod remained. Vegas loved preferential treatment, VIP service. It loved room service and lavish buffets, renowned chefs and crowded cafes. It loved stretch limousines to exotic cuisines, but also loved fleet-footed valets. Parking garages were such a maze.

When Mom moved to Vegas, she had no one to meet her and no one to open doors. She still had her looks and her charm, but at her age it wasn't easy making waves—even in a town that loved a splash.

Mom loved cities from NY to LA, from tall to sprawl. My sleepy beach town was much too small. She wanted more than flip-flops and surf shops and volleyball, more than a fifties throwback where the meter maid met the mermaid at the sea wall.

When Mom kissed me goodbye at the bus station, the thermometer read a cool double nickels. Vegas doubled it. Stepping off the bus, Mom slapped on splashes of sunblock. SPF 30 kept her from burning, but not from melting. Without a car, without a job and without a place to stay, she felt the heat as she walked down Fremont Street with luggage in hand and her trigger finger on the classifieds.

Packing triple-digit heat, Vegas summers rode tall in the saddle. Smoking-hot temperatures rose as high as high noon, as high as a spooked stallion. The two-fisted, double-barreled heat had Vegas under the gun and sweating bullets. Even after sundown, temperatures remained as high as a ten-gallon hat.

Over the years, Glitter Gulch had lost some of its glitter and some of its glamour. Eventually, more than silver and gold sparkled on Fremont Street—including discarded wine bottles—which reflected the dark side as well as the light. Now, along with the glitter and the glitterati came the litter and the obliterati.

As luck would have it, Mom found a place on Thirteenth Street. The landlord took to her instantly and gladly opened doors. They were not the doors to fortune and fame, of course, nor did she expect otherwise. On the other hand, she did not expect to sign a short-term lease only to spend the next twenty years in fabulous Las Vegas.

The same old same old had never been her cup of tea. Give her a city of broad avenues and cobblestone streets steeped in diversity. Mom was not one to keep on keeping on, to chew a stick of gum after the flavor had gone. If a slot machine didn't hit, she moved on.

If Mom did hit a jackpot, she spread it around. "Better than giving it to the doctor," as she put it. And she would know. Her father had diabetes, lost everything to diabetes. It robbed him blind.

As the card slappers, the lip smackers, and the wisecrackers played blackjack, Mom chewed Black Jack. It was her gum, and video poker was her game. She also played the slots, but always played within her means. Mom never counted on house money to pay the rent.

Quarter machines took a minimum bet of one quarter or two bits, as they used to say. Mom always played the maximum of five quarters or ten bits. It didn't increase her chances of winning, but if she did win, it greatly increased her winnings. Mom was more than a two-bit player.

Visitors swamped Vegas like a summer monsoon. They poured into spacious hotels and pored over expansive menus. Food and lodging could be had for next to nothing back then, but visitors still walked away with next to nothing. What they gained at the table, they lost at the tables—in spades.

Long after mom passed away, her image still spilled from my head like coins from a loose slot. Her words came back too. Like a cherry payback, they were not lost on me.

# The Cowboy and the Clown

Mom loved the mountains dressed in sunlight from morning to night. She loved their latest look as the sun turned from red to yellow to white. She loved Red Rock to the west, ravishing in morning's light; and Sunrise Mountain to the east, gray at first light to blonde beauty in broad daylight.

She loved the full moon risin' over the horizon, like Mother Earth giving birth. She loved the stars so bright—a gaga moment—like Oscar night. She loved the cactus that took a stand in the sinking sand and the tortoise that survived day and night at any Fahrenheit.

The desert was a land of silence and stillness, of sand and sun, of spiders and snakes and scorpion. It was a land of extremes—of nightmares and daydreams—of nighttime's starry canopy, but not a blade of grass for a grasshopper to defy gravity.

Vegas stirred slowly under a fiery sky. The day promised to be as warm as toast and just as dry. Passing clouds were a flash in the pan, and then they were gone. The sun came up sunny-side up after the crack of dawn.

Mom loved the arid land, trim in turquoise sky and khaki sand. She loved how Vegas dressed, except that layer of smog worn like a vest. From the Fremont Street cowboy to the Circus Circus clown, she loved both the well-heeled Strip and well-worn downtown.

As the winds of change swept over the Strip, downtown drew a line in the sands of time. Shrimp cocktails were only seventy-five cents, penny candy still a dime. Mom loved downtown from the Union Plaza to what have ya. She loved the magic and the charm and the abracadabra, but the Strip had her under its spell. It could really razzmatazz her.

Mom loved the Great Southwest with its wide-open spaces and topless skies, its shifting sands under the shifting sun. She loved her day in the sun, her moment to shine in space and time.

# Inn for the Night

I left San Diego by headlight. There wasn't a dog barking or a stereo stereotyping, blasting the same old same old. The waves tossed and turned, but the city slept soundly to the restless sea.

Three hundred miles later, Paradise Square apts basked in morning's glory. Olives hung like jewelry from the tree beside Mom's balcony. The day was calm and clear, as inviting as could be. It must have been seventy.

I arrived at eleven and at the eleventh hour. The minute hand had just eclipsed the hour hand, crossed in front of it, and hid it from view. Mom was not visible either. Ordinarily, she would have been out on the balcony and eagerly awaiting my arrival. She used to joke that I should have driven for Greyhound. I was always on time.

At the front door, I knocked repeatedly. Finally it opened. Mom greeted me, as usual, with her wonderfully warm smile. She was all gussied up, as she liked to say, looking forward to having Thanksgiving dinner at one of the hotels along the Strip. Moments later, she plotzed down into the adjacent couch.

Mom had no energy. Crossing the room was a chore. A trip to the mailbox was a trek. A walk in the park was no walk in the park. Getting ready that morning must have taken hours.

Her spirits were good. She didn't carry the weight of the world on her shoulders, but she couldn't get the lead out of her shoes. Mom was dragging. She had always been active. Now she rarely went out. When she did, it wasn't for long. By three or four, she was in for the night.

Weeks earlier, seeking answers, Mom traipsed from one appointment to another—one disappointment to another. Eventually, a cardiologist pinpointed the problem. Her heart was giving out. Without an operation, which she refused, it would fail.

Along with the grim prognosis, the doctor urged Mom not to fly. The stress of takeoff and landing, however mild, could be the last straw. The warning did more than highlight the gravity of her condition. Mom loved air travel, and the thought of having her wings clipped was almost as dismaying as the diagnosis itself.

Mom wasn't going very far anyway. Soon a trip to the supermarket would be out of the question. Pushing a shopping cart up and down the waxed aisles was taxing enough. Asphalt turned the parking lot into a tar pit.

Arthritis brought Mom to her knees years ago, and a recent bout of pneumonia knocked the wind out of her sails. Both sapped her strength, but the arthritis was a given and the pneumonia cleared up. Her latest malady had her down for the count.

Through it all, Mom had no one to advise her, no one in her corner to show her the ropes, no one to dab the cuts and the jabs, no one to assuage the emotional blows. She had no one to take her and no one to bring her home. No, she had no one waiting as she bobbed and weaved her way from waiting room to waiting room, test to test, specialist to specialist.

I hardly had time to unpack on that Thanksgiving morning before hell came crashing down. One minute Mom was sitting comfortably on the couch. The next minute she was fighting for her life. Paradise Square had descended into Hell Square.

The Grim Reaper must have been waiting to show off his handiwork until I arrived. I watched in horror as he pried and pried, separated body from soul until Mom died. To have had her gizzards gored or to have been cut to ribbons by scissors and sword could not have been worse than what she endured.

The ticking time bomb within Mom went off with dreadful force. Twice it detonated, and twice it rocked her like a rag doll on a hobbyhorse. Back and forth and back again, the Richter scale would have registered a ten.

Sitting with head arched back, her mouth opened and closed—gasping, gasping, gasping—desperate for the oxygen that a broken heart could no longer supply. With eyes rolled back, her hands opened and closed—grasping, grasping, grasping—desperate for a life already lost.

Her last breath was just the start, deprived as she was of her heart. She could not see or hear or taste or smell—only suffocate—in that living hell. Compounded by each moment that came before, she suffered more and more the closer that she came to life's last door.

For many years, my mother's heart beat like a drum. It beat to the mamba and the samba and the cha-cha-cha. It beat to the 33 and the 45, the four-track and the eight-track, the cassette, and the CD. It beat to the singing bird, the whistling wind, and the steady rain. All the world was a cosmic dance, and every day her heart beat to another song until the day that brought the siren's song. On that day her heart beat no more.

# A Scattering of Ashes

Red Rock Canyon was twenty miles from the Strip, but could have been twenty light-years. It was another world. Its chiseled cliffs paralleled the Strip, but not for long. While they painted the horizon red, Vegas painted the town red.

Vegas had cash and cachet. It was a gambling town and knew how to play—to roll the bones, as they say. Red Rock had no bones to shake, rattle, or roll—no dice—and made no bones about it.

In Vegas, time flew by like a throw of the dice. Time took its time at Red Rock, like paradise. Unlike Vegas, which concealed its age, Red Rock revealed its ages. The lines, the cracks, the crevices on the face of its cliffs were a dead giveaway.

Life was hard at Red Rock, as hard as a rock. While Vegas loved wine, women and song, Red Rock stood silent—stone silent. Vegas had the gold, but Red Rock had the grit. Vegas had games and gaming, playoffs, and payoffs. It also had snake eyes, but not like those at Red Rock.

A lone hawk circled overhead at Red Rock. Dragonflies darted to and fro. A purple thistle drew blood. Red ants trickled past like blood. The guests, as such, had arrived and the ceremony, as such, had begun. A few flowers, a few words, a few tears and it was all over.

Now Mom was in the hands of the sun and the sand, the wind and the rain. She was twenty miles from the Strip, but could have been twenty light-years. She was in another world.

After graduating from prep school at the bottom of his class, the author spent the next five years earning a degree in sociology, which he never used. It did, however, keep him out of the draft. The Vietnam War was raging, and a student deferment was all that stood between him and the jungles of Southeast Asia.

Upon graduation, that quickly changed. The selective service snatched him up like found money. Fortunately or unfortunately, while waiting to be drafted, he had a brush with the law. It wasn't much, but it was enough to designate him as "morally unfit" to serve. After that, finding a good job proved challenging. If the army didn't want him, who did?

He ended up volunteering at a co-op for one-dollar-an-hour food credit. After about a month, they put him on the payroll. He never left. As the produce buyer, experience taught him to carry local whenever possible. That included excess fruits and vegetables from members' gardens. As such, shopping at the co-op was like having a thousand backyards.

www.ingramcontent.com/pod-product-compliance
Lightning Source LLC
Chambersburg PA
CBHW022118150726
47990CB00003B/1405